Jumpy

April De Angelis's plays include *Wild East* (Royal Court), *A Laughing Matter* (Out of Joint/NT/tour), *The Warwickshire Testimony* (RSC), *The Positive Hour* (Out of Joint/Hampstead/Old Vic; Sphinx), *Headstrong* (NT Shell Connections), *Playhouse Creatures* (Sphinx Theatre Company), *Hush* (Royal Court), *Soft Vengeance* (Graeae Theatre Company), *The Life and Times of Fanny Hill* (adapted from the James Cleland novel), *Ironmistress* (ReSisters Theatre Company), *Wuthering Heights* (adapted from Emily Brontë's novel for Birmingham Rep) and *Amongst Friends* (Hampstead Theatre). Her work for BBC Radio includes *Visitants*, *The Outlander*, which won the Writers' Guild Award 1992, and *Cash Cows* for the *Woman's Hour* serial. For opera: *Flight* with composer Jonathan Dove (Glyndebourne, 1998), and the libretto for *Silent Twins* (Almeida, 2007).

also by April De Angelis

APRIL DE ANGELIS: PLAYS I
(*Ironmistress*, *Hush*, *Playhouse Creatures*, *The Positive Hour*)

A WARWICKSHIRE TESTIMONY
A LAUGHING MATTER
WILD EAST
AMONGST FRIENDS

APRIL DE ANGELIS

Jumpy

faber and faber

First published in 2011
by Faber and Faber Limited
74–77 Great Russell Street, London WC1B 3DA

Reprinted with revisions, 2012

Typeset by Country Setting, Kingsdown, Kent CT14 8ES
Printed and bound by CPI Group (UK) Ltd, Croydon CR0 4YY

All rights reserved

Copyright © April De Angelis, 2011

April De Angelis is hereby identified as author
of this work in accordance with Section 77 of the
Copyright, Designs and Patents Act 1988

All rights whatsoever in this work, amateur or professional,
are strictly reserved. Applications for permission for any
use whatsoever including performance rights must be
made in advance, prior to any such proposed use,
to Casarotto Ramsay & Associates Ltd,
Waverley House, 7–12 Noel Street, London W1F 8GQ

No performance may be given unless a licence
has first been obtained

*This book is sold subject to the condition that it shall not, by
way of trade or otherwise, be lent, resold, hired out or otherwise
circulated without the publisher's prior consent in any form of
binding or cover other than that in which it is published and
without a similar condition including this condition being
imposed on the subsequent purchaser*

A CIP record for this book
is available from the British Library

ISBN 978–0–571–29912–6

Jumpy was first performed at the Royal Court Jerwood Theatre Downstairs, Sloane Square, on 13 October 2011, with the following cast, in order of appearance:

Tilly Bel Powley
Hilary Tamsin Greig
Mark Ewan Stewart
Lyndsey Seline Hizli
Frances Doon Mackichan
Roland Richard Lintern
Bea Sarah Woodward
Josh James Musgrave
Cam Michael Marcus

Director Nina Raine
Designer Lizzie Clachan
Lighting Designer Peter Mumford
Sound Designer Paul Arditti

The production, produced by Royal Court Theatre Productions and Ambassador Theatre Group, transferred to the Duke of York's Theatre, London, on 16 August 2012, with the same creative team and the following cast, in order of appearance:

Tilly Bel Powley
Hilary Tamsin Greig
Mark Ewan Stewart
Lyndsey Seline Hizli
Frances Doon Mackichan
Roland Richard Lintern
Bea Amanda Root
Josh James Musgrave
Cam Ben Lloyd-Hughes

Characters

Hilary

Mark
her husband

Tilly
their daughter

Frances
Hilary's friend

Lyndsey
Tilly's friend

Bea

Roland
Bea's husband

Josh
their son

Cam
a student

JUMPY

A teenage girl, Tilly, walks across the stage. She is dressed in a short skirt, heels, bright colours. She is listening to an iPod.
   We hear the music: Florence and the Machine.
   She does not see her mother, Hilary, who watches her, tired, carrying two shopping bags. Hilary puts down the bags, takes out a bottle of wine, screws off lid and pours herself a glass.

ONE

Mark and Hilary.

Mark So you got on the Tube?

Hilary Yes.

Mark You took the escalator down?

Hilary Yes.

Mark And you weren't thinking anything in particular?

Hilary Nothing. Except –

Mark Except?

Hilary Nothing.

Mark It must have been / something.

Hilary No. / Well.
   I was remembering the time I took the dog to Hyde Park. For some reason I couldn't remember the rules

about dogs and escalators and I thought, Christ I'm going to have to carry it.

Mark He wouldn't have liked that.

Hilary No. He wondered what the hell was going on. He hadn't left ground level for a considerable number of years. It was a nightmare. I was sweating, the dog was doubting.

Mark That's what you were thinking this morning?

Hilary Yes.

Mark You got on to the Tube, sat down. And then.

Hilary It wasn't immediate. It starts with a random thought. I don't want to tell you what it is in case it's viral.

Mark Tell me. I'll be immune.

Hilary There's this thought that there's a lot of earth above my head –

Mark I wouldn't think that.

Hilary – that I was in a tunnel bored deep down.
And above me earth, heavy, dark, between me and –

Mark The top.

Hilary Yes.

Mark Air.

Hilary Yes.

Mark Outside.

Hilary Yes. And this feeling became.

Mark What?

Hilary It reached a level
 Of panic
 Which was unbearable
 And I thought if I don't get off this train –

Mark What?

Hilary I'll die.

Mark That's not good if you have to go to work every day.

Hilary I know. It's shit. It took me two and a half hours to ride five stops. After work I had to get a cab home.

Mark How will you be tomorrow?

Hilary No idea. Might try my bike. Stress.

Mark Yes.

Hilary Job stuff.

Mark Yes.

Hilary Worst-case scenario it happens to us both. Your business bottoms out. I get made redundant. And there are fuck-all jobs out there.
 There's no point worrying.
 Fifty sounds too old to put on an application form.
 I might lie. No one would know. I don't look fifty.
I don't act fifty. I could get away with forty-three. Don't you think I could get away with forty-three?

Pause.

Mark Depends.

Hilary On?

Mark If the person you're talking to happens to be forty-three they might think you look a little older.

Hilary What's the likelihood of saying I was forty-three to a person who happens to be forty-three?

Mark Quite high.

Hilary What would it have cost you, Mark, to say I look forty-three? If it made me happy?
Would it have cost you the earth?

Mark It'll muck up your CV. You could drop a year, two at most. What's the point?

Pause.

Hilary What time is it?

Mark 8.18.

Hilary Are you going to walk the dog?

Mark Yes. I'll take it round the block.

Hilary We don't work in car plants. Didn't mind when they went – too many cars on the road anyway, melting the icecaps, but a bloody Educational Reading Support Unit. How dare they?

Mark It might not come to that.
Don't think about politics when you get on the Tube.

Hilary She has no idea.
We mustn't tell her.

Mark What?

Hilary Anything. Telling her stuff like losing our livelihoods will only destabilise her further. Give her more fuel for disturbance to turn into her own brand of exquisite torture to inflict on us, her parents.
What I'm hoping, Mark, is that what happened today was just a wobble.

Mark I think it is.

Hilary You know what else I was thinking? That time we took Tilly and her friends down to Brighton for the day right at the end of primary school and in the back of the car they were playing a game. They closed their eyes and took it in turns to tickle the inside of each other's arms, wrist to elbow, and Tilly said that's the equivalent of a quarter of an orgasm.

Beat.

Would we have said that when we were eleven? I wouldn't. An orgasm.

Beat.

Hilary You'd still have been playing with your Scalextric.

Mark I may have looked like I was playing – I was cognitively developing.

Hilary Where are you going now? I'm still talking.

Mark Dog.

He exits.

TWO

Tilly, Lyndsey (pregnant), Hilary.

Lyndsey Hello, Mrs Winters.

Hilary Hello, Lyndsey. Call me Hilary. I'm a Ms actually, anyway.

Tilly Ms. Like the sound you make before you vom.

Hilary Well, that's who I am.
  Goodness, look at you, Lyndsey. When did that happen?

Tilly You want to know *when* it happened?

Hilary No, I didn't mean –

Lyndsey Lloyd Park, 10.30 p.m., September 2nd 2008. I remember everything because.

Hilary What?

Tilly Nothing. Is it your business?

Pause.

Hilary Your boyfriend. Is he still – involved?

Lyndsey No.

Hilary That's a shame.

Lyndsey He would be, but he's dead.

Hilary Dead?

Tilly Mum, I don't really think she wants to talk about it.

Lyndsey It's all right. I've come to terms with it.

Tilly It's cool of Lyndsey to keep this baby because Keiron got stabbed.

Hilary Oh God.

Lyndsey His mum's pleased. It's something to look forward to.

Hilary Well, I'm really sorry, Lyndsey, what a lot to go through. That's awful.

Pause.

What about your GCSEs?

Lyndsey I'm taking them this year. Then a year out then I'm going back to college.

Hilary Good. As long as it's your decision. The baby.

Tilly Who else's decision is it going to be?

Hilary I always remember you, Lyndsey, from the school plays.
   The Lion King. You stood out. A hyena.

Tilly It's Lyndsey's decision.

Hilary I'm just saying there might have been pressure on Lyndsey, that's all, to keep it. It's not inconceivable.

Tilly Keiron got another girl pregnant as well. And she's having hers – so it was Lyndsey's choice.

Hilary Keiron fitted a lot in.

Tilly He died, Mum, it's not funny. At the bus station, Walthamstow.

Hilary Yes, I remember seeing all the flowers.

Lyndsey Me, his mum and his sister went down there every day. We used to hurry down there like we were late to meet someone. Stupid. In the end the council took them all away. The bouquets. When they went brown.

Hilary Perhaps you and this other girl expecting his baby, could be friends, support each other?

Tilly God no, she's got a monobrow.

Hilary What's that got to do with it? What she looks like? What A-levels do you want to do, Lyndsey?

Lyndsey A BTEC in Beauty Therapy.

   Pause.

Hilary Well, people always want to be beautiful.

Lyndsey I'll be able to fit work in round having a kid.

Tilly Let's go.

Hilary Where are you two off to?

Tilly The Oak.

Hilary What is the attraction of that place?

Tilly Cheap booze.

Lyndsey It's my birthday.

Tilly Sweet sixteen.
   There's loads of us going. And some guys from Forest School. I'll be really late.

Hilary I'll pick you up.

Tilly We're getting the night bus.

Hilary You've got GCSEs in a month. Don't forget.

Tilly A month. Yeah. I can't stay in every night like you.

Hilary Watch your drinks. Don't let anyone put anything in your drinks. You can have two drinks.

Tilly Down there they're too mean to waste drugs on other people.

Hilary It's not going to be people you know. Ruby, the woman that walks Pete's dogs, it happened to her – she woke up in a hotel room – had no idea how she got there – Rohypnol.

Tilly All right!

Hilary Well, it happens.

Lyndsey No one would bother to drug me, I'm too fat.

Hilary You're pregnant, / not fat.

Tilly Let's go.

Lyndsey Couldn't lift me.

Hilary Have a wonderful birthday, Lyndsey.

Tilly Laters.

Hilary Good luck.

Lyndsey Thank you.

Exit.

Hilary Tilly!

She returns.

Have you got any money?

Tilly I won't be buying the drinks.

Hilary Who'll be buying them?

Tilly shrugs.

(*Giving her some money.*) Take this – buy your own. And buy one for Lyndsey. A soft drink. Give me a hug.

Tilly I can't.

Hilary Why didn't you tell me about the baby?

Tilly I did.

Hilary Was she using contraception?

Tilly God. Please. I don't want to hear you say that word.

Hilary Be careful. Have fun.

Tilly Bye.

Hilary Do you think she really wanted to?

Tilly What?

Hilary With that boy, Keiron?

Tilly Don't be gay.

Hilary I'm fine with you going out but it has to be balanced by work because you need, you need –

She has gone.

Exams.

THREE

Hilary and Frances.

Hilary Lovely to see you. You're looking wonderful.

Frances You too. We got that over with – now can we have a drink?

Hilary I love this. Our second Friday of the month. A great institution.
 What I thought we'd do is just drink and eat crisps.
 If we get desperate we could order a pizza.
 I've been getting those rocket pizzas.

Frances Fast delivery.

Hilary Cheeseless, lightly strewn with a kind of plant growth.

Frances The guilt factor of pizza and the brownie point of a green salad. You sign up for something you don't really get, sounds too much like my life.

Hilary You know we mustn't fall into that trap.

Frances What trap? Why haven't you opened a bottle?

She opens a bottle.

Hilary This is what we do every time. It's like we're wound up and plonked down and there we go down the same route. What year is it? It could be last year. Any year. We have to stop whingeing.

Frances I'm not going to sit here being positive. That would be insane.
 I got on a train the other day with a writer.

Hilary Yes?

Frances Used to be an actor – we'd been in a show together years ago. He was 'beyond gender' in his work, he was telling me. That's all right for him. He's a bloke. Gender is burying us alive. Old women. Our only chance is to run a country or some vast significant organisation like Sainsbury's. That's all that's going to save us from invisibility. Being a woman and getting old is a disaster.

Hilary Don't be defeatist. No one's saying it's easy.

You had that availability check. David Hare play. What happened with that?

Frances They never saw me. Checked my availability and when they found out I was available they thought, God, no. If no one else wants her, we don't.

Hilary They didn't do that. That's just negative thinking.

Frances I went up for a film the other day. A war thing.

Hilary Great.

Frances To play an ageing German prostitute.

Hilary Right.

Frances I won't get it. There were a host of us dressed as old tarts just panting for the part. The bus home had its moments.

Hilary Did you finish your decorating?

Frances Yes.

Hilary Aren't we going to talk about it?

Frances No.

Decorating is false consciousness. You think you're improving your life, you're slapping paint on walls.

Hilary No, I don't accept that. In the seventies they painted everything white. A new start.

Frances The seventies were brown and orange. Most people weren't even born then.

The seventies – no one bothers with it now.

Hilary Rubbish. The woman's movement. Glam rock. Do I have to go through a list of our achievements?

Frances attempts to balance a glass on her head or does some writhing movements.

What are you doing?

Frances Something interesting. You're being boring.

Hilary I'm biking to work now, did I say?

Frances Good for the arse.

Hilary It also gets me to work.

Frances Get any comments?

Hilary No. Fortunately.

Frances Pity.
 I used to love that. Being a young woman being sexy on a bike.

Hilary You hated that, we both did.

Frances I thought I hated it, I was wrong, now I miss it. I wouldn't get on to a bike now. I'd get withdrawal symptoms.
 I was in a bar the other night. Being witty, laughing, being absolutely bloody brilliant actually. The stuff I was coming out with – I wish I could have recorded it for posterity. You know you get those nights.

Hilary Well –

Frances And I was getting admiring glances. I could feel that. On the surface of my skin.

Hilary You can't feel that.

Frances A woman's second sense, come on.
 I was looking fucking amazing too. What a package. I never let myself go.

Hilary Neither have I.

Frances Persevered with vaginal toning.

Hilary Never top of my list.

Frances This man my age, looked older, and not as attractive as me, OK though, worth a punt, I could sense him at the edges of my force field being drawn in by my verbal magnetism.

Hilary Really?

Frances So when it was time to take a waz I walked past him, bit of a squeeze, packed bar. Thought I'd give him the full impact of my many charms at close quarters. I smiled, looked him straight in the eyes. Dead. Not so much as a flicker. Total reptilian blank. Or rather – actual distaste.

Hilary Well, you didn't know anything about him. Maybe someone he knew had just died?

Frances Yeah, that's what I do when I get news of a death, go straight to All Bar One.

Hilary It doesn't matter.

Frances No. Fuck him.

Hilary Yes. Some tossy / estate agent.

Frances Contracts lawyer. It does matter.
  I haven't got a pension.

Hilary Got the flat.

Frances I've always thought of sexual attractiveness as an extreme fallback position. If I was starving. Do I look better like this?

Holds the sides of her face – like a facelift.

Hilary You look more surprised.
  You're having some kind of crisis.

Frances It's called being fifty. You must be having it too.

Hilary No. Actually. Definitely not. No. No. There's more to life. You know.

Frances Going to a gallery – evening classes.
Feels like someone's stolen something from me.
But I don't want to hog. Your go.

Hilary Did I tell you about the other day?

Frances What?

Hilary When I came home and found – well – Tilly was home from school.
I'd got back early. She was supposed to be revising. She was just sitting there on the sofa and when she saw me come in her face changed but I ignored that because I couldn't see a reason for it so I pushed it to the back of my mind and then down the stairs came this boy.

Frances A boy?

Hilary Fifteen years old. Both of them. They'd nipped home – found a 'window'.
To be honest I actually felt sick.

Frances Well, they're all so lush, aren't they? Flawless and bursting with hormones.
What was he like, the boy?

Hilary In his boxers. Tall, skinny. Hair hanging over his face. He grunted.

Frances I love that look. They haven't become men yet. Does he play the guitar?

Hilary I didn't ask.

Frances Let them get on with it.

Hilary She was letting me know she wanted my help. She wanted me to find out.

Frances Doesn't sound like she needed any help. Young love. I'm bloody jealous. Is it ever that good again?

Hilary Of course it is.

Frances The best we can expect of life now is avoiding the worst. I'm scared.

Hilary Scared?

Frances holds out her glass.

Frances Wine. I don't like looking ahead. Do you?

FOUR

Roland This is terrific, isn't it, Bea?

Pause.

We really appreciate you taking the time. I'm sorry we've got such a short 'window'.

It's . . . we've had this . . . dinner planned for – well, it's a shame.

Hilary That's fine. Honestly. Thanks for seeing me at such short notice.

Roland Great, great. We've got forty-five minutes.

Bea Less than that.

Roland Well, yes, a bit less, you're right.

Bea The traffic.

Roland Yes.

Bea Thirty-five minutes. More like.

Roland Well, let's crack on with it then.

You did the right thing. Didn't she, Bea? We completely understand.

Bea Well –

Roland What?

Bea We don't think as one, Roland.

Roland We understand. That's what I'm reassuring Hilary about.

Hilary I just thought it needed attending to –

Roland Totally. We love Tilly . . . She's a lovely girl. Feisty. But polite. Well done.

Hilary I found them. I came home that day earlier – they were both there. Tilly and Josh. They were truanting. And it was obvious . . . that they'd been –

Bea It was obvious? Why?

Hilary Because they weren't wearing any clothes. He was in boxer shorts, Tilly was in an old shirt.

Bea It doesn't mean they'd had sex.

Roland We're not arguing. We agree they did. I thought Josh was looking bloody pleased with himself. I wasn't having sex when I was fifteen. Lucky sod.

Bea You have no idea.

Roland Of course. It's serious. But there are no bones broken.

Hilary Tilly told me later. I asked her and she said yes. They'd done it three times.

Roland Coffee?

Hilary No, thank you.

Roland I think we've taken our eye off the ball where Josh's concerned. I think we have to hold up our hands and say that. We've both had a lot on. Bea's at HSBC. I'm an actor. I've been horribly busy.

Pause.

What do you do, Hilary?

Hilary I'm in literacy. I manage a reading support unit. We work in schools. We see quite a few troubled teens.

Roland You know what you're talking about then. Obviously.

Bea Josh isn't troubled.

Hilary Tilly's on the pill now.

Roland Christ, she wasn't before?

Hilary No. Well, fifteen.

Roland No, no.

Hilary I feel we somehow need to monitor the situation.

Bea You mean keep some sort of chart?

Roland Of course not. She doesn't mean that.

Bea It's happened. It's done. There's nothing we can do now.

Hilary If they sleep together I want it to be at our house.

Roland Right.

Hilary It's just a way of containing it – sex means big emotions.

Bea It's the same for Josh.
What if we said it can only happen here, for Josh, for the 'emotions'?

Roland But we're not saying that.

Bea Are we saying it's different for girls than boys? How Victorian.

Roland It is different. Isn't it?

Hilary It's a big thing for Tilly. I'm her mother. It doesn't hurt Josh to realise that.

Bea They like each other a lot. They've explored their sexual feelings. They've gone on a journey together.

Hilary I think Tilly's in love.

Roland I expect Josh is too. Only he's a bloke.

Bea What does that mean?

Roland Well, he won't know he is.

Bea Josh is very different from you, Roland. For a start I'm his mother.

Roland Well, look, let's not get on to, on to my mother.

Hilary So perhaps you could let Josh know.

Bea I don't feel comfortable doing that.

Roland I'll do it. Look, it's fine, we're agreed.

Bea It feels punishing.

Hilary It's about taking responsibility.

Roland It's fine. It'll be fine.

Bea You don't know that. You're taking something that's natural and saying it needs to be supervised.
   It's not Josh's fault.

Roland No one is saying it is.
   I mean, I think we have to hold up our hands here, Bea, and admit that boys want it more, at that age.

Bea That's nonsense. Total unreconstructed.

Hilary I think that probably is nonsense.

Roland OK, I give in.

Bea I have to go and get changed.

Hilary Of course. Thank you for seeing me. I realise it's a shock for you too.

Bea exits.

Roland Everything will be sorted.

Hilary I'm her mother – you understand. Because really it's not the same for girls.

Roland I've never been a girl.

Hilary They have approximately three thousand images of airbrushed-over sexualised women pumped out at them every day.

Roland That is awful. Unless you're a bloke.

Hilary They feel they have to be sexual to be human.

Roland Oh yes, yes, yes.

FIVE

Tilly Why did you go?

Hilary Look.

Tilly What's it got to do with you?

Hilary Look.

Tilly It's got nothing to do with you.

Hilary Yes it has.

Tilly I'm sixteen.

Hilary Not for a month.

Tilly I can't believe you did that, you ruined my life.

Hilary Don't overreact. Don't be stupid. How could I have ruined your life?

Tilly They won't have liked you. What did you wear?

Hilary I don't know.

Tilly You didn't wear your jeans?

Hilary I don't think they cared what I wore. It was what I had to say that was important. What's wrong with my jeans? Aren't I allowed to wear jeans any more?

Tilly I'm just saying that was the worst thing you ever did.

Hilary Listen –

Tilly You had no right, no right to do that.

Hilary You'll see it differently soon.

Tilly I won't.

Hilary In a year even.

Tilly No.

Hilary When you're my age.

Tilly I'll be dead by then.

Hilary Don't be ridiculous.

Tilly When I'm that old.

Hilary Well, you say that now, that's what everyone says, but life's very precious, I can tell you. No one says, 'Oh, I'm a bit old, I have a grey hair, I'm finishing it all.'

Tilly I will.

Hilary I said to them that I'm happy for you and Josh to see each other but you're both fifteen and I want it safe, I want it here and I think actually he'll respect you more for that.

Tilly It's finished.

Hilary When did that happen?

Tilly When you ruined it.

Hilary When did that happen?

Tilly His name's all over my Humanities folder. It really hurts.

Tilly exits.

Hilary Don't slam the door like that. Tell me. Tell me. What is so appalling about the idea of me in jeans?

SIX

Bedroom.
   Hilary's phone beeps. She checks it.
   She gets into bed beside Mark.

Hilary *Great Expectations?*

She picks up a book.

Where were we? Pip's met Mr Pumblechook.

Mark I think I'm going to sleep.

Hilary We'll never get through it at this rate. If you keep falling asleep. At night.
   Immediately, like this. I could just read a page.

Mark What's the point? I'll be asleep the minute I close my –

Hilary Christmas. That's how long we've been reading this. We reckoned a couple of months. It's July. We're defaulting on our project.

Mark Don't call it a project.

Hilary Project is a good word.

Pause.

Projects stop you being bored. I used to be so scared of boredom as a kid I had a kind of phobia about it. Like I feared being thrown into a living grave and trapped there for eternity. Did you get that feeling?

Mark No.

Hilary Lucky you. We lived in a flat. You had a garden. Maybe that had something to do with it, being trapped in a flat with a depressed mother.

Mark Maybe you were an odd kid.

Pause.

Night.

Hilary I wasn't. The sixties. The dark ages. Women in nylons and stilettos. That's how my mum picked me up from school when it was snowing.

Her only concession to the arctic conditions was a headscarf. Femininity must be asserted over everything, even frostbite.

Pause.

Are you asleep?

Mark How could I be asleep? You're talking.

Hilary It's interesting though, isn't it?

Pause.

I told you about our core funding.

Mark Yes.

Hilary We haven't got any.

Mark You thought it might go.

Hilary It's still a shock when it does.

Mark You'll have to crawl up the arse of the commercial sector.

Hilary I'm not looking at it that way, Mark. That's a predictable way to go.

I'm heading down the road of creative partnerships.

Mark Excellent. Goodnight.

Hilary How's your work?

Mark It's not picking up.

Hilary I got a text.
From Tilly. She's bringing Josh back.

Mark To stay?

Hilary Yes.

Mark I want to go to sleep.

Hilary They're back together. Thank God. Which is good for Tilly.

Mark I don't want to hear anything.

Hilary You won't hear anything. There are walls. Walls.

Mark Goodnight.

Hilary Walls between us. Solid walls.

Pause.

You'd have to be really listening out for –

Mark All right.

Hilary You know, really listening.

Sound of two young people walking past the room and going into the next-door room. Laughter. Muted talk.

You can hardly hear a thing. The good thing is we have a wardrobe against that wall. Full of clothes. Muffling everything. A happy accident.

Quite loud creak of bedsprings.

I could hear that. Could you?

Another creak.

We have to let them know. We have to – if we laugh – they'll know we can. Come on.

She looks at him, she laughs.

Mark What are you doing?

Hilary Laughing.

Mark Laughing like a lunatic.

Hilary If you weren't going to join in, why didn't you let me know? Of course it sounds strange to laugh out loud when the other person is totally silent. Do you want him to think I'm eccentric?

Mark Who cares what he thinks?

Hilary He goes to Forest School.

Mark So what?

Hilary He's a nice boy. If he likes us – he'll be kind to her.

Mark He better be kind to her – He's in there –

A loud creak.

Hilary Well, this isn't the nineteenth century.

Mark We never brought girls home when we were fifteen.

Hilary Sixteen now.

Mark Whatever. We fumbled about in the cinema.
We waited till university to have full sex. It was all part of the learning experience.

Is it respectful – to bring back – into the next room – next to your parents?

Hilary Shh. They'll hear us talking about them.

Mark Don't tell me to shh in my own house.

Hilary Shh.

Another creak.
　She starts to laugh.
　He starts to laugh.

Mark What?

He reaches out for her.

Hilary No, no. What if they hear us?

He is hurt.

Mark We're not doing things right.

Hilary This is what happens now.

He turns over. Shuts his eyes. Hilary turns out the light. Creaks in the dark.

SEVEN

Roland, Hilary.
　A silence. They both speak at the same time.

Both I do.

Laughter.

Roland It's a mess.
　You must have felt something.

Hilary I think I was so caught up in –

Roland Yes, what you were –

Hilary Yes.

Roland But you could sense something? I felt as if it was blaring out of loudspeakers. These people are in meltdown.

Hilary I couldn't tell. Most couples appear to be on the verge of – some kind of dissatisfaction.

Roland Yes, that's very good. Yes.

Pause.

So after you came to see us – about the kids – I felt we hadn't told you everything.

Because we were in trouble – and he was reacting to us.

Hilary Josh.

Roland Yes. A kind of rebellion.

Hilary That makes sense.

Roland That's what he was telling us with Tilly. A kind of 'fuck you, I'm a man now'.

Between me and his mother it hasn't been good. I mean that's tangible. And then when I waded in and said – it's fine, but do it at Tilly's house, he walked away from it all – but really I was the one he was rebelling against because it was me telling him.

Hilary But it's OK now. They've sorted it out.

Roland Teenage boys and their fathers. Freud was right. Underneath it all they'd like to eat us and take our women.

Hilary They don't know how to cook, do they?

Roland You don't need to cook warm flesh. You just need sturdy teeth and a lack of consideration for others. Most teenagers qualify.

Hilary 'I only have a short window.'

Roland We made that up. About the window. I said to Bea, people know when you're lying. They just know instinctively. Did you know?

Hilary No.

Roland There goes another theory. Soon I'll be left with nothing.

Hilary Was there something specific?

Roland I could murder a drink.

Pause.

We, I, felt bad about what happened next. But it was when it was really hitting the rocks. I couldn't speak to Bea without shouting. I've moved out. Now I live with the sofa bed and our old kettle. Everything's crappy.

Hilary What 'happened next'?

Roland I said to Bea we should have told you.

Hilary What?

Roland Josh was really upset.

Hilary What about?

Roland He was with another girl and they were at a party.

Hilary Whose party?

Roland They're always at parties. And Tilly came – as far as I can make out he didn't know she was going – she didn't know he was – and then she went up to a bedroom with a guy – and then after that another guy . . . she was angry with Josh.

Hilary Oh God –

Roland I've been wanting to tell you. Josh told Bea. He was gutted.

Hilary When did this happen?

Roland Over a month ago – right when Bea and I were going through it.

Hilary She never told me.

Roland Well, you can understand that.

Hilary I'm her mother.

Roland I wouldn't take it personally.

Hilary Why didn't she tell me?

Roland It's OK. She's probably talked about it to her friends. They like their friends better than us. We like them better than our friends. That's OK. They move in packs. Day and night – every minute they want to be with each other. Can you imagine wanting to spend that much time with other people? I mean a few drinks, lunch, an evening. But every minute of the day? Phoning, eating, sleeping at each other's houses, they can't get enough. What happens to us that we grow so un-enamoured of each other? People turn your stomach, don't they? Their fucking issues and their vanity.

One minute there's the nappies, the Calpol, their inconvenient sicknesses, reading them the same story till it's tattooed on the back of your eyelids – though Bea did that mainly – you can't wait for them to go to sleep at night so you can get in a few glasses of wine – then this redundancy. How does that happen?

Hilary I'm not redundant.

Roland Maybe with girls it's different.

Soon we won't be parents. I'll say 'my son' and I'll be referring to some twenty-eight-year-old lunk who works for a living. That actually gives me a pain.

Hilary We shouldn't hurry time.

Roland Bea accused me of flirting with you. I told her she was being a maniac.

Hilary Like who would?

Roland I didn't mean that. I told Bea I was being friendly. I'm a tactile person.
And warm. I'm an actor, for God's sake, I don't know how to turn off the charm, that's how I make a living.
Where's Mark?

Hilary Scotland, visiting his mother.

Roland Didn't fancy it?

Hilary I didn't want to be poisoned. Every jar in the fridge is more than two years old.
She has a hardened immune system. Visitors aren't so lucky.

Roland That's what's in store for us all: mouldering. You have nice skin.

Hilary Clarins. I can't afford my skin.

Roland Bea had nice skin. It was her personality that stank. Am I genetically divorceable?

Hilary ?

Roland Do you think that sooner or later anyone would have ceased to love me? What am I talking about, 'love'. 'Like' would have been good enough. I would have put up with 'just tolerate long enough to sit down to dinner with'.

Hilary It doesn't sound like you've been having a very good time.

Roland Did Bea seem a little caustic to you?

Hilary I don't know. Maybe.

Roland Or just frigid? I was a fucking eunuch in that marriage. Am I repulsive?

Hilary I don't know. No.

Roland If I did flirt with other women can you blame me? I was literally starving in that department.

Hilary Was she having an affair?

Roland No. Why? Have you heard something?

Hilary No. No.

Roland I used to lie next to her, my whole flesh weeping to be touched. All I got was, 'You need to take a look at the bathroom grouting.'

Hilary It's odd what goes through your mind.

Roland She was punishing me for some crime I never committed. Being in a marriage with her.

Hilary Men have greater survival rates in marriage.

Roland Surviving. Is that what I've been doing?
So how's your marriage?

Hilary It's fine.

Roland Don't fucking lie to me.

Hilary I mean obviously we're not – in the first throes of passion – it's not like it was.
We tend to lead separate lives. A bit.

Roland Go on.

Hilary I suppose I'd be scared not to be in it.

Roland Thank you.

EIGHT

Hilary and Tilly.

Hilary How was school?

Tilly All right.

Hilary Did you have a good day? Tell me something that happened.

Tilly Christ, I just walked in the door.

Hilary Don't go upstairs yet.

Tilly Why?

Hilary Just sit down, have a cup of tea with me.

Tilly No.

Hilary Five minutes is all I'm asking.
I want to talk to you.

Tilly God.

She sits down.

Go on then, speak.

Tilly's phone goes. She gets it out and reads a text, laughs. Texts back. Hilary waits till this is over.

Hilary Having a daughter, well, it's a privilege.

Tilly's phone beeps again.
She scans phone. Texts back quite a long message. Hilary waits till this is finished.

It goes fast, though, really fast, and I don't want to waste this time we have together.

Tilly Is this going on much longer?

Hilary Why?

Tilly Because it's really dull.

Her phone beeps. She answers.

Hilary Can that wait?

Tilly No.

Hilary Of course it can. It can't be more important that this.

Tilly Well, it is.

She texts back.

Can I go now?

Hilary SIT DOWN!

Tilly Don't go all psycho on me.

She sits.

Hilary I want us to do more things together.

Tilly Like what?

Hilary I wanted to show you my album.

Tilly What album?

Hilary The blue one. I stuck everything in. Old bus tickets.

Tilly What's a bus ticket?

Hilary / What's –

Tilly I know. / Joke.

Hilary There's photos of me when I went to Greenham Common.

Tilly What?

Hilary A peace camp
A protest against American nuclear missiles being sited at Greenham. Women lived there.
For years. In tents. I went. It got very muddy.

Tilly Like Glastonbury without the music.

Hilary There I am.

Tilly Why are there are loads of men there?

Hilary They're women. They have short hair.

Tilly Not a good look.
Can I go now?

Hilary In December 1982 thirty thousand women from all over Britain came to 'embrace the base'.
Which we did. Nine miles of perimeter fence. You felt this incredible energy and also lots of confusion, women were saying, 'Are we supposed to hold hands now?'

Tilly Time's up.

Hilary I'm talking to you.

Tilly Five minutes, you said.

Hilary I didn't mean five minutes.

Tilly You're a liar then because that's what you said.

Pause.

Hilary Is there something you want to tell me?

Tilly What?

Hilary Something you want to tell me?

Tilly No.

Hilary Are you sure?

Tilly What?

Hilary I know what happened at the party.

Tilly What party?

Hilary The party where you went into a room – and – did you use a condom?

Tilly Oh my God.

Hilary We have to talk about this.

Tilly I'm sixteen. I don't have to talk.

Hilary No, I know. But if you want to.

Tilly I don't want to.
What's the matter with you?
Why don't you have a drink?

Hilary Listen.

Tilly Open another bottle.

Hilary I have two glasses a night.

Tilly Yeah.
I'm going out.

Hilary You're not.

Tilly I'm not a prisoner.

Hilary It's a school night.

Tilly It's six o'clock.

Hilary Twenty past.

Tilly So. I'll be back in an hour.

Hilary Is that the three-hour-long hour?
Or the four?

Tilly Is this talking?

Hilary Let's not shout. This is emotional.
All I'm saying is – be safe, look after yourself. That's all I'm saying. Tell me.

Tilly What is it you want me to do? Do you want to tell me what to do?

Hilary Listen. You think 'I'm being a strong woman', that's a misinterpretation . . .

Tilly Like you're so happy.

Hilary What?

Tilly You heard.

Hilary It's never an hour, is it?

Tilly It's never five minutes, is it?

Hilary But did you want to do it?
What did you want?

Tilly Did I want?

Hilary Yes.
You must know. What you wanted?

Tilly LEAVE ME ALONE.

Mark enters.

I want to go to Lauren's for an hour.

Hilary She wants to go out. Tell her she can't go out.

Mark Hello.

Hilary Just tell her.

Mark How long for?

Hilary It's a no.

Tilly An hour.

Mark OK. That seems OK. If it's an hour. That should be OK.

Tilly exits.

Bit of an overreaction.

Hilary She slept with some boys at a party. She hasn't told us.

Mark Hold on. Hold on. What?

Hilary That's it. That's all I know. Look at us, we're supposed to be a family.

She exits.

37

NINE

A beach
  Roland tampers with a shop-bought, for-one-use barbecue pack.
  Hilary enters.

Hilary Have you lit a fire before?

Roland I must have, I'm a man. I think with these it's just a matter of – firelighters. I can do that. A woman could do that. This was such a great idea. Inspirational. Thank you. Why is Frances so desperate?

Hilary She's not.

Roland She directs everything she says straight at me. Like bad acting.

Hilary She's good at connecting with new people.

Roland She wants me.

Hilary You should be so lucky. She's good at sex. She takes charge. She has toys.

Roland Are you trying to shunt me sideways on to your friend? Because it's you I like, not her.

Hilary Yes, but we're not going to happen. I'm married to Mark.

Roland But you told me –

Hilary What I told you . . .

Roland You didn't love him in that way.

Hilary We're outside.

Roland You said you were just going through the motions. For Tilly's sake.

Hilary You're very needy. Your marriage is over and you're grasping at me. My marriage is held together by habit, but that's OK.

Roland When you came to see me and Bea, I thought there's a woman that has passionate convictions.

Hilary Stop talking like this. You're making me anxious.

Roland Are you scared to leave Mark – because your job's on the line?

Hilary I'm trying to remember why it is I like you.

Mark walks in with a cool bag. He has on shorts and a T-shirt.

Mark I'm fatter than I was last year. Look.

He grabs his tummy.

Roland You should sort yourself out with a longer T-shirt, mate.

Hilary Too short. Doesn't cover the top of –

Roland Then your spare tyre wouldn't –

Mark This is my favourite T-shirt. Darts. 1979. World tour. Winchester.
 I'm not eating more – some fats cells moved in and thought, this is good, this is permanent – we must tell our friends. And this process of accumulation is taking place independently of any responsibility on my part.

Roland Is Frances after me?

Hilary Don't assume she's out to get you because she's single and over forty.

Roland Fifty, isn't she?

Frances enters in a bikini, sunglasses.

Mark That's brave for Norfolk in September.

Frances Any chance to get my clothes off. I've only got five years left in this body.

Mark Then where do you go?

Frances It's hard to attribute mortality to me, I know I'm a goddess, but the decline of musculature is relentless.

Hilary Stop it.

Frances Then the ears lengthen, noses grow longer and the jawbone loses material.
 Our faces collapse.

Hilary Think Meryl Streep. We need a new attitude. Our lives are written on our bodies and our faces. Our experience. Who'd want to be a blank? Think of all the stories we have to tell each other?

Pause.

We have so many stories.

Roland Is it too early for alcohol?

Frances I thought you'd never ask.

Mark opens up the cool box, takes out beer bottles, distributes them.

I'm stunned with inertia when people tell me stories. And there's only one thing worse than hearing a boring story once and that's hearing it twice. There's an old girl at the home I do shifts in – she's always asking 'What's that called outside?' 'Winifred, it's the corridor!.' I get so desperate to get back to people in basic working order I have to will myself not to run away screaming.
 It's coming to us all.
 (*To Roland, who has a towel round his waist.*) Don't keep us guessing. What have you got on under that?

Roland Trunks.

Frances Can't wait. Did you buy them yourself?

Roland My ex-wife bought them.

Frances You see this is my theory: only an older man would buy a young woman swimwear. (*To Hilary.*) I bet Mark never bought you yours, did he?

Hilary No.

Frances What's under your jumper then?

Hilary God, just an old costume.

Frances Let's see.

Hilary I'm not that warm actually.

Frances Not shy, are you?

Hilary We don't all get time to go to the gym like you do. I've been helping Mark out in the shop every spare moment.

Frances How is the world of blinds?

Mark Slow. As it happens.

Frances Blinds was an odd turn for you to take, wasn't it? I was just thinking. For an art student.

Mark Needs must.

Pause.

Frances (*to Roland.–*) So, how is detoxing after decades of marriage?

Roland You're not one of those mad women who don't respect boundaries, are you?

Frances Yes.

Roland I thought so. It's pretty shit, actually. I was levelled. I was the shit on your shoe. There was no time of day I looked forward to.

Frances I've been there. It lasts about two months.

Roland Four in my case. Then I progressed to the taking-it-out-on-my-liver phase. Occasionally I'd have a few hours when I felt normal. Then it kicked in all over again. When I found out Bea was seeing someone else, I felt as though a knife was plunging into my groin . . .

Hilary The local lifeboat crew are singing *a cappella* tonight in the Grapes.

Roland I thought emotional pain was a metaphor till then.

Mark Where are the kids?

Hilary I woke them up. They should be here now.

Frances Did you get it checked out?

Roland What?

Frances Your prostate?

Hilary I shouted at them through a closed door – I think they heard.

Roland It was a metaphor.

Mark They'll still be sleeping.

Hilary I didn't go in – obviously.

Roland My balls were in perfect working condition, which was part of the problem.

Mark Pity for them to miss so much of the day.

Hilary You wake them up then.

Roland Getting sexual favours out of my ex-wife was akin to chipping at a glacier with a toothpick. I'm honest about that. Most people lie. Then it makes it harder for people like me to come out. You put up with abstinence because you think it's just you. You don't know it's practically every married couple in the Western hemisphere.

Hilary Are we going to swim?

Mark Swimming, in England. That's novel.

Hilary Who wants to be sluggish?

Frances I applaud you, Roland, for your honesty.

Hilary Let's go in. Come on.

She takes off her jumper. She is wearing a light-coloured costume – a bit risqué.
The teenagers, Tilly and Josh, enter. They look like gods.

Roland Hello, you two.

Tilly Oh my God, Mum, that's disgusting. You're practically naked. Put something on.

Mark Mum looks fine.

Roland Very good. Morning, Josh.

Josh makes an inaudible reply.

Frances That's not an old costume. You've gone out and bought that, you sex bomb. It's a flesh tone. That's why it looks so undressed.

Hilary puts her jumper back on.

Hilary Bit cold for swimming.

Tilly You can look now, Josh. It's safe.

She looks at package of fish.

Ugh. Josh doesn't like fish.

Roland Don't you, Josh?

Hilary There's salad.

Tilly That's not food.

Hilary begins to get out the food.

Hilary I don't want you going funny about eating.

Roland Josh will eat anything.

Hilary Wonderful.

Tilly No, he wouldn't. He wouldn't eat a rat. He wouldn't eat another man's penis. Like that bloke near us who ate his friend's. They cooked it first.

Roland Obviously.

Frances God, it all happens in Walthamstow.

Hilary Why don't you try it? At least try some fish.

Tilly I've tried it. It's rank.

Hilary It's dieting that makes you fat.

Tilly You're always going on about your fat arse.

Mark *and* **Roland** She hasn't got a –

Hilary Anorexia is a mug's game.

Tilly Oh my God. We're going for a walk.

She exits. Josh follows her.

Frances Oops.

Hilary Mark. I was about to get her to eat fish.

Mark That was never gonna happen. Let her walk it off.

Frances Is she always like that?
I don't know how you put up with it.

Hilary Well, that's the thing, with children you can't take them back and exchange them.

Frances She's lovely, really

Roland They have a lot of stuff we never did but they don't seem to like us more for giving it to them.

Frances My niece has a mobile, an iPod, driving lessons, a laptop. We had record players and people shouting at us to get off the phone.

Mark I used to play with a stick.

Roland Josh has six hundred and sixty Facebook friends. How many have you got?

Hilary Ninety-eight.

Frances Tragic.

Roland They don't need us.

Mark They may be angry with us. We're responsible for them being here.
  It's dawning on them, as they look at us, it's not going to be a fairy tale.

Hilary You never stand up to her, Mark. I look like the bitch.
  I'm going in.

She exits.

Frances That's why I never had children.

Mark I'll start the fish.

Roland They sleep the sleep of angels, you know.
  No two a.m. horrors. Sometimes I lie there –
  Wondering which is the next bit of me that's going to fall apart – I'm morphing into an old geezer. A hairy back, balding legs. Like an ostrich.
  (*Looking in direction of Tilly and Josh.*) I wonder where they've gone.

TEN

The cottage, five p.m.

Tilly Why aren't they back yet? Josh pulled his 'help me' face as the car drove off. Why can't they just buy wood from a shop?

Hilary They wanted an experience with nature. Maybe you should have gone with him. Got some exercise.

Tilly Join the nightmare.

Hilary Being with his dad is not a nightmare.

Tilly Why does he say it is, then? I had stuff to do.

Hilary Urgent stuff like bleaching your non-existent moustache.

Tilly It's not non-existent. I inherited it from you. Only I have more pride.

Pause.

Am I going to get those things round my eyes? Like you've got?

Hilary What things?

Tilly Like you've been attacked by a cat.

Hilary Yes. They spring up overnight aged about sixteen. Try not to lose any sleep over it.

Tilly When are you two going away?

Hilary We are away.

Tilly Together. For a weekend. Without me. A week? Sacha's parents are always going away. They went to St Petersburg. She has great sleepovers.

Hilary Sorry. Not on the horizon. We're in Norfolk. Let's just enjoy that.

Tilly You and Dad would have such a good time. Get the old love-juice flowing, Dad. You know you want to.

Mark The Van Goghs in the Musée d'Orsay. We got to them half an hour before it shut and we weren't even looking for them – just stumbled into this gallery. Genius paintings.

The portrait of Dr Gachet. Holding these healing herbs. Hallucinatory colours.

Hilary (*to Tilly*) Dr Gachet was . . .

Tilly I don't care.

Mark I could do that again.

Hilary Look what you're doing. Giving in to her. She just wants us away so she can have a party.

Tilly Sleepover.

Hilary We'd come back, our loo would be pulled off the wall.

Mark I wasn't giving in. I was thinking aloud.

Tilly Forget it, Dad, she doesn't want to go with you.

Hilary I don't like the idea of coming back and having no place to shit.

Tilly Your definition of home.

Roland and Josh enter.

Roland I just need to –

Josh His eye –

Hilary What happened?

Roland No fuss – I just need to –

Hilary Your eye?

Roland Ridiculous.

Josh Wood chip bounced into his eye. Bang on target.

Hilary Is that dangerous?

Roland A scratch –

Josh gets out his BlackBerry.

You're not –?

Josh Googling it.

Roland That's unholy.

Josh 'Many people are discovering the adventure of chopping wood. But even for the experienced woodsman or woodswoman the possibility of injury or even death should be taken into consideration for this seemingly simple task.'

Roland What – when I accidentally chopped at my own neck?

Josh 'Even the smallest piece of wood, flying off can cause major injury to the eye and medical attention would be needed almost immediately.'

Roland I can't listen to this. It's written by a fool who wants everyone to stay indoors.

Josh The Forestry Commission.

Hilary Let me see. Get a torch, Mark.

Mark exits.

Roland Just need to bathe it.

Tilly Josh. (*She indicates to him.*)

Hilary I'll see to it.

He goes.

Roland I was just trying some father–son bonding.

Maybe I'll lose an eye. All this liberal shit – we should just beat them senseless.

That's what my father would have done.

Mark re-enters
Hilary shines the torch into his eye.

That's hellish.

Hilary I can't see anything.

Roland Let me – get some water on it. It'll be fine.

Roland exits.
Frances enters.

Frances You know that thing I was telling you about?

Hilary No.

Frances Yes, that thing I've been going on about relentlessly for weeks only you've obviously just been pretending to listen.

Hilary Oh yes, that.

Frances Well what do you think?

Hilary Well, it's your call.

Frances (*to Mark*) I want to try this thing out, Mark, on some mates, it only takes five minutes, what do you think?

Mark Is it a starter?

Frances No.

Mark Well, fine.

Frances Good. I'll get ready.

She exits.

Mark Don't you want to go to Paris?

Hilary I have to start the dinner.

Mark Don't you want to go to Paris with me?

Hilary Can we afford it?

Mark With me?

Hilary God, do you want to do this now?

Mark What's the point?

Hilary What?

Mark The point in us. Is there a point?

Hilary Mark –

Roland comes in with a handkerchief held over his eye.

Roland 'You should have seen the other fella.'

Mark exits.

You like my jokes. With Bea they fell on stony ground. I can talk to you so easily.

The sound of my voice used to grate on Bea's soul. I could see her flinching. If we were having a dinner party and I launched on an anecdote – you have to do that sometimes at dinner parties, otherwise all you hear is that dreadful clicking of knives on plates – she should have been grateful to me – instead I could see something slide down behind her eyes.

She was postponing her life until after I'd finished and someone else, who wasn't her husband, would say something that might kindle a fire in her.

She was a fucking effigy.

Hilary You're not over her.

Roland I'm getting there. You're warm. Not like Bea. Bea looks like a woman, got the right bits, but she's a hemale. Don't be fooled by her people skills, it's every woman for herself as far as Bea's concerned. Can we have some booze?

Hilary White's open.

Roland I'd kill for a red.
  I did sleep with other women. By the end. It was a survival thing. And I was quite surprised. These lovely young women, interested in me.

Hilary Right.

Roland That's why life is so . . . You feel like shit and then – something can happen between people. The space between you becomes charged – all the little emotional tentacles reaching out. Imagine living without that.

Hilary Flirting.

Roland It's being alive and not being old.

He moves towards her.

Hilary How is the eye? It's quite red.

Roland Good when it's looking at you.

He touches her face. Moves away as Tilly and Josh enter, followed by Mark.

Tilly We need a lift to the station.

Mark Wait. I said it needed a discussion first.

Hilary No. No way. Dinner's in an hour.

Tilly If we don't go now there'll be no point. We'll miss the train. Chloe's sister's having a party. In Islington!

Hilary Out of the question, sorry.

Tilly Dad says we can. It's going to be really good.

Mark No, that's not correct. I said a discussion.

Hilary Why did you say that? That just gives her leverage.

We're away. For the weekend. What's so difficult to understand about that?

Tilly Yes, but we don't like it.

Hilary None of us like it, that's not the point.

Tilly Dad.

Hilary Say no to her for once.

Tilly We're bored here. You don't even really want us here.

Mark Sorry, love, it's a no. It's not so bad here with us?

Tilly It's marginally better than being dead.

Roland We can go for a walk after dinner. Josh, remember those great walks we had in France?

Josh I was eight. You lost me. It was pitch black. I almost fell into a river.

Tilly Please. We're dying here. It's so dull. It's just wine and talking.

Hilary No. What's wrong with you? It's a no.

Tilly (*to Mark*) Why do you always do what she says?

Frances (*off*) Can you do the music for me?

Tilly She doesn't even like you.

Frances (*off*) The music.

Tilly She treats you like shit.

Frances I'll switch it on, then.

She switches the music on.
  And performs a burlesque routine.

Black leather, black balloon. Challenging.
Quite a lot of it directed at Roland.
She finishes, switches off the music.

I'd love some feedback. What did you think?

Roland I can't see any more. Both my eyes appear to have swelled up.

Frances That's an extreme reaction.

Hilary Oh God.

Roland Who said that?

Hilary Oh God.

Roland No. I know –

Josh It's your eyes, Dad. You should take it seriously.

Hilary (*to Mark*) Drive him to Casualty.

Roland It's actually fucking terrifying. Will I go blind? Oh Christ. It's a Greek tragedy right here in Norfolk.

Josh You're going to be OK, Dad. We're taking you to Casualty.

Tilly Can you drop us at the station after?

Mark Yes, love.

They start to exit.

Hilary (*as Mark leaves*) What are you doing? Does anything I do have an impact on anyone? Is anyone listening to me? No, Mark, I don't think there is a point.

He exits.

Frances Well, that was a resounding yes. What did you think?

Hilary I wasn't really concentrating.

Frances It's quite empowering about female sexuality. I'm definitely in control.

Hilary Do you think the kids should have seen it?

Frances I think it's an antidote to the pornographication of women. I control and playfully manipulate the gaze. The only thing was my balloon burst too early.

Hilary Yes, there's glitter all over the floor. Like there's been a party.

Frances exits, leaving Hilary alone.
Roland re-enters.

Roland I told them I needed a piss. I'm not blind yet. The walking wounded.
  I wanted to –

He kisses her. They kiss.

– feel like I'm fifteen.

He exits.

ELEVEN

Hilary with a glass of wine.
  Tilly and Lyndsey, looking remarkably glamorous and sexy.

Tilly We're going now.

Lyndsey Hi, Hilary.

Hilary Lyndsey. How are you? You've had the baby.

Lyndsey Yeah.

Tilly He's really cute. Dayne.

Hilary I'd love to see him.

Tilly She'd love to get her hands on him.

Lyndsey He's really nice.

Tilly She's got baby envy.

Hilary No, I haven't.

Tilly No, of course you haven't – baby lust. One little peek at his little fatty arms.

Hilary How's life, Lyndsey? We don't see you that often.

Lyndsey It's OK.

Hilary You're looking well.

Lyndsey Thanks.

Hilary Really wonderful.

Tilly She's such a skinny minny.

Hilary So where are you off to?

Tilly Town.

Hilary Stick together, won't you. Where?

Tilly This club Lyndsey's sister goes to.

Hilary What's it called?

Tilly You won't know it. Fabric.

Lyndsey It's got a bodysonic dance floor.

Hilary Has it? What's that?

Tilly Music pumping from the floor.

Lyndsey It goes through your whole body. Pumps through.

Hilary That sounds good.

Lyndsey It's really sick.

Hilary It sounds – sick. What sort of music does it play?

Tilly Mum. Don't be such a freak.

Hilary Do they let sixteen-year-olds in those places?

Tilly We have fake IDs.

Hilary Do you?

Tilly Got it online, twenty quid.

Hilary Right. Why don't you have a drink with me here first?

Tilly We're meeting people.

Hilary One glass.

Lyndsey They can wait ten minutes.

Hilary Least it'll be decent wine.

Hilary pours.

Lyndsey My sister hangs out with a footballer.

Hilary Do footballers go to this club?

Lyndsey I got an itinerary, where they all go. I downloaded it.

Hilary Is that what you want to do, Lyndsey? Meet a footballer?

Lyndsey Yeah. I'll get him to pay for my lipo.

Tilly Lyndsey wants lipo.

Hilary Oh my God, you don't.

Lyndsey I do.

Tilly Don't set her off.

Hilary You've got a beautiful figure.

Tilly It's no good, she wants lipo.

Lyndsey My fat legs.

Hilary It's a surgical procedure. It has a risk factor. You can't encourage your friend to have lipo, Tilly.

Tilly I'm not encouraging her.

Hilary You were never supposed to have a Barbie.

Tilly Oh my days, not this again.

Hilary I always swore you never would and then you had a party when you were six
And got given two.

Tilly The happiest day of my childhood.

Hilary Barbie is an Aryan. Put together by eleven thousand Chinese women in Guangdong Province. She's a recipe for self-hatred.

Lyndsey I love your mum, she's so original.

Tilly Let's go.

Lyndsey I heard about you and Mr Winters having a trial separation. I'm really sorry.

Hilary That's OK. Thanks, Lyndsey. These things happen.
Tilly?

Tilly What?

Hilary Life has to be a balance.
Work and play.

Tilly I do work.

Hilary Because things get serious now.
I mean, how you did so well in your GCSEs. You won't get by on that amount of work this time – A-levels are a different level.

Tilly Yes, they're A-levels. It's Saturday night.

Hilary Yes.

Tilly Get a life.

Exits.
Hilary sits drinking alone.

TWELVE

Spring 2010.
  Hilary, Frances.
  Hilary is changing in an adjacent room.
  Frances is dancing and finding songs on the iPod.
  Hilary comes in, wearing a dressing gown.

Hilary I haven't had a 'visitor' for four months. What happens now?

Frances I get myself a glass.

Hilary Is my cunt going to dry up?

Frances Wait till I get a drink down me, for God's sake.

Hilary It doesn't seem that long ago I got my first period. That smear in the crotch of your pants. I ran in to my mother, I said 'I've become a woman.' She looked at me like I was insane. She took me to the bathroom and showed me where she kept her 'towels'.
  Like I was being inducted into a cult.

Frances What did you do for Tilly?

Hilary I gave her a Topshop voucher. She didn't want a fuss.
  I've hit a low point.
  I've let go of too many things at once. Periods, job's on the line, Mark.

Frances In that order? It's not very flattering to Mark, is it?

Hilary It'll be Tilly next, then I'll be alone. I'm not sure I want to do this.

Frances It'll cheer you up. Go on.

  She ushers Hilary into adjacent room.

There was a picture of Kim Cattrall in the papers the other day, a full body shot and then a close-up of her chin, she has a sagging chin and it said – even Kim cannot fight off the advancing years.

Hilary (*off*) Sexist tossers.

Frances And then I got to thinking. She's got the money – why doesn't she sort it out?

Hilary (*off*) So would you?

Frances Definitely.

Hilary (*off*) You could die. Under the knife. Like that woman that wrote *The First Wives Club*, Olivia . . . She was having her chin done. Maybe, you know, Kim wants to live.

Frances Come on. Let's have a look.

Hilary enters. Burlesque costume.

Hilary I don't like it.

Frances Therapy.

Hilary It's not working for me.

Frances Performing is a powerful place to be.

Hilary I just can't see myself doing it.

Frances Amateur night. You needed something. You were a mess. This is my suggestion. Please take it seriously.
We'll find you some music. You acted at university.

Hilary *The Duchess of Malfi.*

Music: Helen Reddy's 'I Am Woman'.

What is that? Post-feminist irony?

Frances Try the moves. (*Giving advice.*) Stick out your arse more. Try being suggestive with the duster.
I've just about forgiven you for the Roland thing.

Hilary What?

Frances I was in there with a chance. We had so much in common.

Hilary You weren't in there with a chance.

Frances Well, you would say that, that's your moral justification.

Hilary Nothing's happened, after that one time, he's all talk.

She breaks off.

It's making me want to cry.

Frances You liked my routine.

Hilary That thing you did in Norfolk? I was uncertain.

Frances And how's Mark?

Hilary Well, he's still living above the shop.

Frances Basically you've got two men sniffing around you and you're at my throat for considering a facial procedure. How unsympathetic.

Hilary Don't let's do this. Don't let's argue. Then we don't speak for weeks and one of us has to pick up the phone and eat dirt.

Frances I blame our mothers.

Hilary What for?

Frances That thing yours said to you.

Hilary What?

Frances She got pregnant with you and so she had to marry –

Hilary Before the pill it was a nightmare – imagine, medieval.

Frances Still a cow. Told you you'd ruined her life. Said that in cold blood.

Don't know why you stood there and took it.

Hilary She's my mother, what could I do? Terminate the friendship?

Frances They gave us their love with a nip of poison. No wonder we hate ourselves, hate women.

Hilary We don't. I've changed the whole dynamic with Tilly.

Frances Yeah.

Hilary What?

Frances Like I've noticed how amazingly you get on.

Hilary This isn't working for me. It feels like a step back.

Frances I knew you were going to say that.

Hilary It's posh people's lap dancing. Frances, what's happened to us?

Frances Us?

Hilary Feminists. Where have we all gone?

Frances We died out, like bus conductors. God, we were pious. Hairy pits and an embargo on mascara. The worse thing was not being able to loathe other women.

Hilary Don't dismiss us. We stood for something.

What am I, the last one standing? When we were at Greenham common –

Frances We did a few day trips. Let's be clear – we weren't really a part of –

Hilary Because we were students. But we were part of – something bigger.

Didn't you feel –
Powerful? Kids' clothes sewn on to the fences.

Frances Thirty years ago. Your point is?

Hilary We should be living those ideas.
I don't know if I have lived them.

Frances You're so sentimental. Grow up.

Hilary The practical thing of life is more tricky. But if you take the politics out, what's left?

Frances The interesting stuff.

Tilly enters.

Hilary Tilly. You're back early!

Tilly Yeah.
(*Refers to her costume.*) That's sad.

Hilary Yes, it is. You've let yourself down, Frances, I'm not joining you.

Frances I haven't got time for this.

Hilary I won't become a 'fuck-me puppet'.

Frances I'm ironically deconstructing it.

Hilary I'm worth more than that. We are, Tilly. I'm just going to –

She exits to change.

Frances (*calls*) I won't be the one phoning you. Bye, Tilly.

Tilly Has she gone mental-pausal?

Frances Probably.

Frances exits.
Hilary comes back with dressing gown.

Hilary (*sees Frances has gone*) Oh God. (*To Tilly.*) Everything OK?

Tilly Yeah.
It was boring. Just round someone's house. Wanna watch TV?

Hilary What are we going to watch then?

Tilly switches on TV.

We can have a cuddle.

Tilly sits obligingly and unusually next to Hilary.

This is nice. (*Refers to Tilly's programme choice.*) Not *Half Ton Teen*!
Unbelievably gross and voyeuristic.

Tilly Makes me feel better.

Hilary You have a beautiful body. Just enjoy it – before –

Tilly What?

Hilary Nothing.

Tilly I'm not looking forward to vagina neck.

Hilary What?

Tilly shows Hilary what she means.

Please. Really. That is – no no. God. Vagina neck. That's hateful, can't you see that?

Pause.

Tilly On Facebook.

Hilary What? On Facebook – what?

Tilly There's stuff posted about me.

Hilary What?

Tilly Facebook-slut stuff. Because – at that party . . .

Hilary Oh no. No. Sweetheart.

Hilary goes to hug Tilly, Tilly moves away.

We'll get it taken off. Can you do that?

It's not the boys that get called that stuff. You see how it works.

Pause.

I think you didn't really want to do it.

You were feeling rejected and you were reasserting yourself by saying 'I'm sexy, I'm desirable', but we add up to more than 'being sexy'.

People can be happy with vagina neck! We don't have to be fucked by a man to be human.

Tilly You're making me feel shit.

Hilary Sorry, love. Think next time: 'Is this what I want? Or is it because I want to be wanted, to feel my existence is validated?'

Tilly What? Like I'm going to think shit like that.

Hilary Do you know what validated means? It –

Tilly My period's late.

THIRTEEN

Lyndsey, holding a baby, Roland, Bea.

Roland He's a lovely chap.

Lyndsey Thanks.

Roland What do you call him?

Lyndsey Dayne.

Roland Is that his name?

Bea It's his name.

Mark comes in.

Mark Sorry – Hilary's on her way – work – some kind of crisis meeting.
 Can I get you –?

Bea No, thank you.

Roland (*to Lyndsey*) Keep you up much?

Lyndsey He's very good. My mum helps.

Roland Does she?

Lyndsey Has him Saturday nights, some Fridays, every Wednesday.

Roland A big commitment.

Lyndsey She doesn't mind.

Roland All those late nights. At her age.

Lyndsey Thirty-six?

Roland That is – that is young. Well, that's good of her.

Lyndsey His dad's mum has him every other weekend.

Roland You've got it sorted.
 We could do that.

Bea No, we couldn't.
 It would be hellish to go back.

Hilary enters.

Hilary Thanks for coming. Lyndsey, your input will be really useful. Is Tilly still –?

Lyndsey Upstairs. I'll text her.

Hilary I haven't said hello properly. Is Josh –?

Bea Josh isn't coming.

Hilary Right.

Bea I've told him he doesn't have to.

Roland You told him not to.

Bea Because it's a bit like a military tribunal.

Roland I don't think it is.

Hilary I thought the idea was to get us all together.

Bea That might be damaging.

Hilary Damaging?

Bea We can give Josh's side of things better than he can.

Hilary Well.

Bea He's sixteen years old. He's still a child.

Hilary But he's old enough to –

Bea The guilt.

Hilary The guilt?

Bea Of this whole – It's designed, unintentionally, to make him feel – guilt.

Roland Make him face his responsibilities.

Bea From the man that had psychosomatic headaches every time I attended a pre-natal class.

Roland I didn't need lessons in deep breathing.

Bea No, that would be me.

Roland (*to Lyndsey*) We've split up. You might be able to tell.

Lyndsey Isn't that weird? You've split up and they've split up and mine's dead.

Roland Yes, that is weird.

Bea The pressure might make Josh agree to something he doesn't really want because –
 He's afraid to say what he really feels.

Hilary I'll tell Tilly not to come down. It's not fair she – On her own.

Bea What are we here for? Look, it's her decision, of course it is.
 Only from my point of view I think it's a disaster for Josh. To father a child at sixteen.
 What kind of father can you be at that age? And not being a good father, what effect does that have?

Roland Are you absolutely sure she's –

Mark We've taken three tests.

Roland So it's highly unlikely.

Hilary I told Tilly you wanted to have input into her decision. And Tilly agreed to get your input. So whatever is decided, she decides – with your input, our input, and Lyndsey's input – but if Josh isn't here, then obviously I can't let her come down alone, it's not fair.

Bea Then how will she get our input?

Hilary You could input to us and we could convey your input to her.

Bea It's more persuasive if it comes from us. This is our son's life.

Hilary She's not coming down if Josh isn't here. Lyndsey, would you mind –

Lyndsey I'll text her.

Roland We thought she was on the pill.

Hilary She was, then she stopped when they stopped and then it started again.

Roland Oh dear.

Hilary I mean, if we had a choice of course –
  I mean, Lyndsey, if you could turn back the clock.

Lyndsey What?

Hilary I thought Lyndsey could advise Tilly – because if you could, Lyndsey –
  Would you choose to have had a baby at fifteen?

Roland It's not that you don't love your baby. But if you could wipe the slate clean.

Bea Look, she's not going to admit to that.

Lyndsey I'm not wiping the slate clean.

Roland No, of course.

Lyndsey Of Dayne.

Roland No no no.

Hilary But in an ideal world of course –

Lyndsey What?

Hilary In an ideal world you might have delayed.

Lyndsey Dayne?
  Then he wouldn't exist.

Hilary He's lovely.
  Yes, in an ideal world, perhaps not for you, but for Tilly – you can see that.

Mark Is she the right person to ask?

Bea Josh has other options.

Hilary Tilly has options.

Lyndsey I have options.

Bea You have less options. Let's be honest. I'm sure you've faced that.

Josh, like a lot of bright kids, has the capacity to go off the rails, to be derailed.

This could derail him. I know it could. The stigma, the confusion of being a child with a child, the adult responsibilities.

Roland Romeo and Juliet.

Bea Are characters in a play.

I don't know why you are seriously giving her an option.

Mark You can't force –

Bea She doesn't understand fully the nature of the decision before her. That should be impressed upon her. I'm not saying forced. How did this happen?

Roland We know how it happened.

Bea I mean how was this allowed to happen? By us.

Hilary By me – are you saying?

Bea Do we think it's OK for girls to be hyper-sexual and not bring upon themselves the, OK, unfair consequences? Josh would be expected to go to a university but as the father of a young child, he won't be developmentally experiencing what he needs – freedom – to learn – to socialise.

Hilary The same for Tilly.

Bea Changing nappies. Wiping up sick.

Lyndsey She says Josh keeps ringing her, can you tell him to stop ringing her?

Bea He's upset.

Roland He should be here.

Bea I don't want him here. It's awful.

Mark We should get Tilly down here.

Hilary On her own, as if she's the guilty one? The girl who dared to have sex – the slut.

Lyndsey She's not a –

Hilary I was making a point, Lyndsey – I wasn't really calling her a –
　I can't force her to get rid of it – she has to want to.

Bea It won't last. Have you mentioned that? The relationship won't last. Perhaps she thinks this will cement something – it's the opposite. Lyndsey, are you with your partner?

Lyndsey No.

All He's dead.

Bea Oh God, yes, sorry.

Lyndsey It's all right. It was last year.

Mark I think Tilly has to be here.

Bea What was he seeking – some kind of love, attention?

Roland He was seeking sex. It's a drive. You missed out on it.

Bea It had a resurgence after you left.
　If it's any consolation, Lyndsey, I'm better off without a man on a live-in basis.
　The benefits are overestimated and possibly an evolutionary disadvantage.

Roland Thank you.

Bea We are happy to pay for the termination privately. That is something we can do.

Mark It's not a question of money.

Bea It's a gesture.
Does Tilly want a baby – at sixteen? Her life will be over.

Lyndsey My life isn't over.

Bea I shouldn't have said over. Severely limited.

Hilary Thank you so much for being here, Lyndsey. Whatever she decides she needs to know how tough it is.

Lyndsey I wouldn't turn the clock back.

Hilary Of course not. You must have feelings of frustration?

Lyndsey I do worry.

Bea Yes –

Lyndsey How I'm going to support him?
Will I meet someone who'll be a good dad to him? When I see on the news – stepdads who *starve* kids, put them in *black plastic bags* in the bath and the mothers stand by, I'm scared, but I won't like anyone like that, will I? Unless I change in some way, get *depressed*, I start taking *drugs*, my life spirals out of control, I end up homeless, a crack-whore – but apart from that I'm fairly positive.
Have you seen that film *The Road*?
The Road made me cry. If someone ate Dayne I'd go mental.
I can't afford to get down. Not now I've got Dayne. Who else has he got?

Bea Your mother. It's just this generation has everything now. Don't wait. We pick up the pieces.
I won't do that.

Lyndsey starts to cry.

Mark We're talking about our grandchild here. We do know that.

Bea We don't know that it is.

Roland Very likely.

Bea There was that other time she – at that party – a stranger. I can't be the only one to be thinking it. It's the elephant in the room. Josh going through all this and it's not his.

Hilary Josh can't just walk away.

Roland No no.

Bea Roland, you asshole.

Hilary Josh fucked my daughter. He fucked her and now he thinks he can just walk away.

Mark Calm down, love.

Bea I'm here to advocate for my son.

Hilary Sorry, Lyndsey, have we upset you?

Lyndsey No.

She holds up her phone.

Tilly. She's been bleeding.

FOURTEEN

Home.
 Hilary is still in her coat. Her knee is bleeding.
 A Young Man walks into the room in boxer shorts.

Young Man You haven't got any milk?

Hilary There's no milk?

Young Man It's cool. I'll have juice.

He pours himself some juice.

Hilary You are –?

Young Man Oh sorry. I'm a friend of Tilly's.

Hilary I'd figured that out.

Young Man Right, yeah. Cam.

Hilary Cam. I don't think I've heard of you. Where's Josh?

Young Man I've no idea. I've never heard of him.

Hilary Tilly's boyfriend.

Young Man Oh yeah – I think that finished.

Hilary When was that?

He shrugs.

Young Man I don't know. Not that long ago. Your house is very hot. We crashed out.

Hilary She never said anything to me.

Young Man shrugs.

Shouldn't Tilly be at school?

Young Man Inset day.

Hilary Right. Shouldn't you be somewhere?

Young Man Uni, reading week.

Hilary Tilly is sixteen – aren't you a bit old for her?

Young Man Twenty?

Hilary Yes.

Young Man It's not like Ronnie Wood territory.

Hilary I suppose not . . .

Young Man He must be well old. Fifty.

Hilary Older.

Young Man Yeah?

He notices her leg is bleeding.

What happened to you?

Hilary I got knocked off my bike.

Young Man Do you want a juice?

Hilary Yes. Actually. That would be good.

He pours her one.

Thanks.

Young Man You ought to clean that up.

Hilary Yeah.

Hilary gets stuff to clean leg.

Young Man I'll do it, if you like.

Hilary OK.

He begins to clean.

I didn't know how thirsty I was.

Young Man Yeah?

Hilary I lost my job today.

Young Man That's a bit shit.

Hilary Yes, it is actually.

Young Man Here's to the next one.

Hilary Thanks.

Young Man You've been having a bit of a *Titanic* day.

Hilary Yeah.

Young Man I don't know your name.

Hilary Hilary.

Young Man Hilary. I saw your photo upstairs.
Tilly told me you were her mum. I didn't believe her. I said you looked too hot to be her mum.

Hilary It's an old photo.

Pause.

What are you doing at uni?

Young Man Psychology.

Hilary What do you want to do with psychology?

Young Man I want to specialise in child psychology. I did a placement in an adolescent unit.

Hilary Yeah?

Young Man Yeah. It was like amazing. There was this kid, he had absolutely no friends. And every time the psychologist asked him a question he just said – yes – like that –
Really fast.

Hilary As if he wanted to stop.

Young Man Yeah, stop any – like –

Hilary Being seen.

Young Man Yeah. It was like he didn't even know how sad he was. He was just tucked into a little ball inside himself. Lost. The psychologist was saying the thing is, he just has to wake up. Somehow he has to wake up. To know how sad he is before he can –

Hilary Move on.

Young Man Yeah.

Hilary Well, that sounds –

Young Man Yeah.

Pause.

Well. I better –

Hilary Yes.

Young Man Thanks for the juice.

Hilary No. Don't go. I mean you don't have to go – yet –

He stops.

Young Man OK.
Did you like your job? I mean, not everybody does.

Hilary I think it's important that people – you know – read.

Pause.

They just opened the car door just as I was . . . the cunt.

She begins to cry but wipes her eyes as Tilly comes down.

Tilly Mum?

Hilary Yes.

Young Man I better –

He goes.

Tilly Cam's helping me revise.

Hilary I'm not stupid.

Tilly What?

Pause.

He is.

Don't take it out on me that you and Dad aren't getting on.

She walks away, turns back.

Oh yeah, and we've run out of shower gel.

Hilary Can't you keep your fucking knickers on? You disgust me.

Tilly turns and exits.

FIFTEEN

Roland, Hilary, Tilly.

Hilary I'm really sorry about tonight.

Roland That's OK. That's OK.

Hilary I hate to think of you sitting in that bar.

Roland It's fine.

Hilary I've been having a crisis with Tilly. I've instituted a new regime.

She's got AS-levels in two weeks.

As far as I know she's done a completely inadequate amount of revision.

I couldn't leave her tonight because – she'd go out. Or be on Facebook.

She wouldn't actually apply herself. The only thing she applies with any diligence is eyeliner. Would you like a drink?

Roland Just water.

She gives him a drink.

Hilary Thought we'd made a breakthrough with *Othello*.

Talking about the women. Desdemona and Emilia trapped on a fort with a load of bastards. But it was a momentary breakthrough. Hostilities have broken out again.

Roland So Mark is –? He's still –

Hilary In the flat above the shop.
I'm going to make a pasta. Ever so simple. I'm sorry. I thought we'd be eating out.

Roland That's fine. That's good. I like pasta. I'd rather be here. I've gone off bars.

Pause.

Hilary So, how have you been?

Roland Rehearsing.

Hilary How's that?

Roland First week wonderful, third week crisis – usual stuff.

Pause.

Hilary How's Josh?

Roland Oh he's – he's OK. Enjoying A-levels. It seems. He went for Drama. That was his mother's genius idea. God knows why. I could have taught him everything he needs to know. Basically, get a good agent and don't take coke.

Hilary I was sorry about Josh and Tilly.

Roland I think it was all a bit of a shock. They wanted to turn their backs on it.
Understandable.

Tilly enters.

Tilly Hello.

Roland Hello.

Tilly Are you gay?

Hilary Tilly!

Tilly We haven't seen that much of you. We thought maybe you've made a discovery. Are you?

Roland No, I'm a Buddhist.

Tilly That's actually more shocking.

Roland I went for that retreat, remember? Down the M3.

Hilary Oh yes. Yes.

Roland I have to say it's really been wonderful. Meditation. I've been working on my Calm Abiding. It's very important go inside and be still.

Hilary I ought to put on the pasta.
Why don't you lay the table?
Could you – please?

She shoves cutlery into Tilly's hands, who begins to lay the table.
    Hilary exits briefly, re-enters.

The Berlin Wall came down over twenty years ago.

Roland Really. That went quickly.

Hilary Yes, I was watching a programme about it. Where does time go?
Do you know what the Berlin Wall is, Tilly?

Pause.

In 1945 . . .

Tilly Nobody cares.

Hilary Well, they might actually. They might have an interest in the world wider than their own wardrobe.

When I was your age I had an engagement with sexual politics.

My vision extended beyond my next outfit.

Tilly I know. I saw the photos. Roland, what do you call a blonde with two brain cells?

Roland I don't know if I should answer that.

Tilly Pregnant.

Roland That is actually quite funny.

Hilary Excuse me.

Roland Can I help?

Hilary I only have to –

She exits.

Tilly She's fucking doing my head in. I'm locked up here with a depressed mother
You like me, don't you?

Roland Yes.

Tilly Can I come and stay with you? I'll just have to throw some stuff into a bag. I'm only asking because I'm really desperate.

Hilary brings in a bowl of salad, puts it on the table.

Tilly Uncle Roland says I can go and live with him in Highgate.

Roland Well I –

Hilary I'm sure he didn't.

Tilly I can stay – he said I could if I packed a bag tonight. We're not getting on.
I can revise there.

Hilary No.

Tilly I knew you wouldn't let me.
You don't know her.
Do you know what she did the other day?
She followed me. She only went and followed me.

Hilary Look, I apologised for that. I overreacted.

Tilly We were walking along and one of my friends pointed and said, 'Look, isn't that your mum in that car?' and I looked and it was – how embarrassing was that?

Hilary This was two o'clock in the morning and her phone was turned off.

Tilly Your own mother like a worm creeping up behind you in a car.

Hilary I was worried about you.

Tilly I'm worried about you – that you're fucking mental.

Hilary You never worry about me, you don't think of me.

Tilly No, because I hate you.

Roland I'm sure you don't.

Hilary They have a gun . . .

Roland A gun!

Hilary A gun.

Tilly Oh my God – that is a joke.

Hilary Tilly was laughing about it on the phone.

Tilly For a joke. No one's going to use it.

Hilary Which is why you are grounded.

Tilly Yes! But it's like the biggest joke – because you can get anything – that is the point – you can get it – it's like

a comment – a social comment, it's like satire. Like men having long hair in your day – or women taking the pill.
　He is not going to use it.
　We laugh. Don't you see?

Hilary No no, I don't see.

Tilly It was a bet. To see if it could happen. To see if Rupert could get one and he did.
　Because you can get anything.

Hilary And you are not leaving this house till I know that someone has handed that weapon to a responsible adult. I've made myself clear. I'm giving them a week and then –

Roland A gun is pretty extreme.

Tilly In Japan they've invented a machine – they can place these electrodes on your head and play you back your own dreams.

Roland Wow.

Tilly Mum would love that.

Hilary Why?

Tilly You always want to get inside people's heads.
　If they invented this injection –

Hilary An injection?

Tilly Like a small microscopic chip that you can't see, a tracking device – because a mobile phone can be switched off – something they inject into the bloodstream – so we can never be lost. So they – a parent – could always know where we are – would you make me do it?

Hilary I think you'd feel really persecuted.

Tilly I bet you would – there's no way you wouldn't.

You would inject your own daughter with some scary technology because you are such a control freak.

Like how fucking sick is that?

Hilary I said I wouldn't.

Tilly Like I believe you.

Roland Maybe, maybe, you know, she's worried about you – she's just being a mother.

Tilly You think that's normal? To think like that? To think the world is such a nuthouse that you need to make your own child into some kind of transmitter?

Hilary This is all hypothesis.

Tilly She'd hunt me down.

Hilary For God's sake.

Tilly You can't control me.

Hilary Upstairs.

Tilly No.

Hilary Don't escalate this.

Tilly LOCKED UP LIKE A PRISONER.

Hilary I GIVE YOU LIFTS, MONEY – CHRIST, YOUR CLOTHES.

Tilly I hope you never get fucked again as long as you live.

Hilary Thank you!

Tilly You're too old anyway. That's what you are, too old.

Hilary Well the world is missing out, that's all I can say. If they can't see what I'm worth.

Tilly OLD OLD OLD.

She exits.

Hilary I'll just check the pasta.

Roland Look, I'm not that hungry. We've got a terrifically long day tomorrow – we're tech-ing. I'll ring you. Come and see the show. Let me know and I'll sort out tickets. Don't leave it too long because the advance is rather healthy.

Hilary Please don't go yet.

Pause.

Roland I feel like – well – I've been so – in such – I've been confused this last year.
 I haven't been myself.

Hilary You don't find me attractive.

Roland No no no, that's not it. Of course you are. Very attractive.

Tilly comes downstairs with a gun.

Tilly See.
 It's Rupert's gun. It's not loaded. I'm not going to shoot you.

Hilary Oh my God.

Tilly It's just a joke. Don't you see? We take turns because Rupert's dad has threatened to stop paying his uni fees if he steps out of line in any way.

Hilary Give it to me.

Tilly No. Look, it's a joke.

She fires it and it goes off.
 She screams. Roland drops to the floor.

Roland I'm OK.

Tilly Oh fuck, that was so weird.

Hilary Drop it drop it drop it.

Tilly Don't freak out.

She drops it.

Roland I heard it go past my ear. A whistling.

Hilary Oh God. You could have killed Roland. Get upstairs and do some revision.

Tilly No. I need to calm down – I almost just killed someone.

Hilary Get upstairs.

She pushes her.

Tilly Don't touch me.

Hilary GET UPSTAIRS!

Tilly doesn't.

Roland Listen. I have to go. Really, it's been –

Hilary You can't go, you've almost been shot.

Roland (*indicates gun*) Post that anonymously to the police. Best thing.

Hilary I'm really, really sorry. Please don't go.

Tilly Don't beg, Mum. It doesn't work.

Roland I really –

He goes.

Hilary (*to Tilly*) Do what you like. I don't care any more.

Hilary exits. Leaves Tilly alone.

SIXTEEN

Cam and Hilary.

Cam Me and Dad used to sit there like ghosts in front of the telly.

The light flickering on his face, and his face was impassive and I was scared to say anything, in case I made him come round.

We spent nights like that. Months. I knew it was wrong but I couldn't see a way out.

Catatonic. That's what we were.

Well, that's life. That's what I told myself. You can't expect everything to work out.

And after Mum died I just thought to myself, well, that will have screwed me up but I'll just have to live with it. It takes ages for the fact that it really happened to sink in. Even now I think – maybe it didn't happen. Cognitive dissonance.

Maybe she wasn't knocked off her bike. Maybe she didn't die.

That's why it was so weird when you came in and you'd been knocked off your bike.

That could have been her, you know, a happy ending.

Mind if I smoke?

Hilary No.

Cam Sometimes I think, maybe it's all some kind of practical joke and one day Mum's going to come giggling out of a cupboard and say 'Got you!' We were a family that played a lot of jokes.

Hilary That's just –

Cam My defences. Yes. Once my dad walked naked into the living room with a rose tied to his penis, only it was my gran. Mum had popped to the shop.

Hilary What must you think of me?

Cam I like you, obviously.

Hilary You must think – I mean this is –

Cam Lost your job, it's thrown you off balance. Blame David Cameron. He's a cunt.

Hilary I'd like to blame him – for this – but I'm not sure it's rational.

Cam I wasn't going out with Tilly.

Hilary I know. But you were in a way.

Cam I wasn't her boyfriend. We hadn't got to that point yet.

Hilary I just wanted –

Cam You really wanted me, didn't you?

Hilary Yes, I did.

Cam I liked that.

Hilary Did you?

Cam Yes.

Hilary I don't think we should do this any more.

Cam All right.

Hilary So that's OK with you?

Cam Sure. I mean, have I got a choice?

Hilary Because that's the best thing. I'm thinking of getting back with my husband.

Cam Look, I can take it. I can take anything after Mum.

Hilary I'm too old for you anyway.

Cam What's the point in thinking like that? You like someone or you don't.
Age doesn't have to come into it.

Hilary That's a good way to think.

Cam Unless you want to have kids. Even now science can do wonders.
That woman who had a baby when she was seventy but then she died of cancer.
Do you want a cigarette?

Hilary No. I gave up.

Cam Poor fucking baby. How weird is that. A test-tube dad and a pensioner mum whose carked it. I mean, who the fucking hell would you be?

Hilary I don't know. I don't want to judge those women.

Cam Pussy. Really irresponsible. Do you want to go for a walk?

Hilary I thought you had an essay to do.

Cam I get restless. Easily.
Well, you've got a nice memory.

Hilary That's a strange way to put it.

Cam How else do you want me to put it?

Hilary I don't know. It sounded a bit punishing.

Cam Yeah?

Hilary Yes.
Why did you come round again?

Cam I left my jumper. I was passing.

Hilary That was convenient.

Cam I thought you seemed – up for it.

Hilary Don't tell Tilly.

Cam State the obvious.

Hilary How did you meet her?

Cam At a party. Months back. It was just after Mum, and we both were destroyed.

Hilary Destroyed?

Cam Booze. And we talked a lot and went upstairs.

Hilary And you?

Cam I cried. Mainly. Yes. Not much else went on. I tried to, but I was too rammed. She said, 'How do you ever get over something like that? Your mum.'

She couldn't imagine getting over it.

Hilary Did she say that? About me?

Cam Yeah. Even though you were an alcoholic.

Hilary I am not an alcoholic.

Cam Teenagers speak in totalities. They don't know grey.

Hilary She said that?

Tilly (*voice, off*) Hello.

Hilary (*indicating kitchen*) In there.

Cam goes into kitchen with clothes, closes the door.

Tilly Forgot my purse, free period.

Tilly goes upstairs.
Comes down.

See ya.

Hilary You don't have to rush home after school tonight. If you want to hang out after. That's OK.

Pause.

Tilly OK.

Hilary I trust you. I'm sorry.

Tilly OK.

Hilary Give me a hug.

They hug.

I think things are going to be fine. Between us.
   What's out there scares me, that's all. I think you're fantastic.

Tilly You don't hate me?

Hilary No, no.

Tilly OK. Laters.

Exits. Goes out without her bag.
   Cam comes out naked with a flower tied to his penis.

Cam That was fucking close.

Tilly re-enters for her bag.

Tilly Forgot my –

SEVENTEEN

Hilary with cigarette, mobile phone.

Hilary Voicemail.

Frances You're overreacting . . .

Hilary She would never do this. This long. Never. Never.

Frances She's angry with you.

Hilary No one would put another human being through this, especially their mother.

Frances Oh, I don't know . . .

Hilary Still not picking up.

Frances There was a lot of shouting.

Hilary Obviously.

Frances Because you snogged this lad.

Hilary It sounds terrible when you say it like that.

Frances I don't know how else to say it.
Fatal Attraction. You ought to watch – Tilly. The competitive thing.

Hilary What?

Frances Snogging her boyfriend. Envy.

Hilary No. Not envy.

Frances Don't kid yourself.

Hilary You never had kids. You don't know what you're talking about.
Anyway, I didn't just snog him, I slept with him.

Frances You didn't?

Hilary Yes.

Frances Whore.

Hilary It's bad, isn't it?

Frances I can't conceive of any possible atonement.

Hilary Really?

Frances No. You were horny and you wanted someone to want to shag you because you're unfeasibly old. She's punishing you. Has she told Mark?

Hilary I don't want her to tell Mark.
She might have done something stupid. Got into an unmarked cab.

Frances She'll be with friends.

Hilary Driven for miles and dumped in a reservoir. Set on fire. Like that poor –

Frances There's no point in going down that route. She's in a club now, dancing to nineties retro music.

Hilary There's a serial killer in Walthamstow.

Frances That sounds a bit glam for north-east London.

Hilary Killed a woman who'd popped out at one a.m. for teabags. Tesco Metro.

Frances Young people move in packs. You told me that.

Hilary You'd think you'd see a woman out with teabags you might have a bit of sympathy. You wouldn't strangle her with her own tights.

Frances A psychopath obviously – 99.8 per cent of men are not like that. He'll be lying low.

Hilary If he's insane he may not be thinking rationally. Can't we move on from bloody Jack the Ripper –?

Phone beeps. Hilary leaps on it.

Mark. Can he come home now?

She punches the keys.

Of course he can't.

Frances Where is he?

Hilary Driving round in a three-mile radius. Searching. I can't bear being in my own skin.

Frances You've rung all her friends?

Hilary Except five of them, we don't know who they are any more. Please don't leave me.

Frances No, of course.

Hilary I can't be on my own.

Frances You're smoking.

Hilary Stopping me from screaming. I could kill her. Why does anyone ever have kids?

Frances Because they're selfish and they don't want to be lonely.

Mark enters.

Mark Two a.m. I'm knackered.

Hilary Are we just going to sit here waiting? We should phone the police.

Mark What are they going to do? It's a teenager – partying at the weekend.

Hilary This is the second night. The second night. This is not normal.

Mark No news is good news.

Hilary Why won't anyone take me seriously?

Mark I'm going to bed. Tomorrow – if – then –

Hilary I know something's happened. I know it.

Mark What happened? Did you argue?

Hilary No. Nothing.

Mark Then we shouldn't panic.

She sits on the floor.

Hilary If something has happened – there's no point in anything.

Frances You don't mean that.

Hilary I do.

Frances She doesn't.

Hilary I'll kill myself.

Frances It was your wedding anniversary today wasn't it? It popped up on Facebook.
Congratulations.

Mark Thank you. We're not – not together at the –

Frances Oh yes. Sorry.

Hilary curls up on the floor.

Shall I make some coffee?

Mark No –

Frances My mother used to flick me with cold water when I got into a state. Like an exorcism. We could do that.

Mark I don't think –

Frances This must be hard for you too. She'll be fine.

Mark Oh, I know.

Pause.

Frances You know my performance that time in Norfolk?

Mark Oh yes?

Frances I've been really working on it.

Mark I don't think now's a good time.

Frances No. I know. No. It's been going really well. The burlesque scene is amazingly vibrant. I've met some really cool women. I've had two actual real live bookings.

Mark I'm really pleased for you. Good luck with that.

Pause. They sit for a long time.

There's no need for you to wait too.

Frances Really?

Mark Yeah. Honestly.

Frances I'd better stay. Otherwise one day she'll hold it against me.

They wait.
  The door opens and in comes Tilly. She is barefoot and carries one shoe.

Tilly Hi. I lost a shoe. Off the pier at Brighton.

Mark Are you all right?

Tilly I needed a new pair anyway. I'm going to bed. I'm so tired.
  Night.

She exits.
  Hilary gets up.

Hilary I'll put the kettle on.

EIGHTEEN

Hilary, Mark. Bedroom.
  Hilary gets into bed.
  Pause.

Hilary That's quite a day. It's strange isn't it? Not waiting for someone to come in.
  How was the drive to the station?

Mark Uneventful.

Hilary I don't think she wanted me to come. I think I made the right decision not to come.

Mark You said goodbye here.

Hilary I offered to go up on the train with her. She said that would be a waste of money. She'd rather have the money.

Mark Well –

Pause.

Hilary I suppose that's considerate. I'm not working. How's it at your work?

Mark Hanging on.

Hilary I expect we'll survive. (*She gets* Great Expectations.) Where were we? Pip. (*She searches through. She stops.*) Then I said to her yesterday, I said, 'Well it's been a bumpy ride, hasn't it?'

Mark What did she say?

Hilary Nothing. She was packing. I mean what do you say? I was starting to sound like something out of *Brief Encounter*. And then I said – 'It's all a journey of self-understanding, of knowing what you want and standing up for it. And that's very important especially if you're a woman.' And that I've tried to pass on those values to her – even though – you know – I'm not perfect.

Mark Yes.

Hilary And she turned to me and she laughed.

Mark What kind of a laugh?

Hilary Well, I was thinking about that afterwards. And I couldn't really – I don't know.

Mark Right.

Hilary I just want her to be all right.

Mark Of course.

Hilary I think she will be. Do you?

Mark Yes.

Hilary As long as she doesn't get into drugs or become the victim of a random terrorist attack or turn into a Tory. As long as she's confident about being a woman.

Mark Yes.

Hilary She will ring us.

Pause.

She took that old toy. That – monkey thing. Jumpy.

And I was really touched that she was taking it because she never used to be able to sleep without it. And I said, 'Oh, you're taking that,' and she said, 'There's this ceremony at Freshers' Week. They light a bonfire and each fresher burns something that represents their childhood. Like a rite of passage. You drink shedloads and then you throw this object on to the fire and watch it burn.' She thought she'd immolate Jumpy.

So I tried to be, like we said, not to be too – to hold on too tight. So I said, 'Well, if that's your decision –' and she said, 'God no, what do you think I am, some sort of sick bitch?'

It was a joke.

Pause.

Are you awake?

Mark Yes, I'm awake.